CW00705125

ANCHOR
BOOKS

A VARIETY OF VERSE

Edited by

Kelly Oliver

First published in Great Britain in 2002 by
ANCHOR BOOKS
Remus House,
Coltsfoot Drive,
Peterborough, PE2 9JX
Telephone (01733) 898102

HB ISBN 1 84418 038 7
SB ISBN 1 84418 039 5

FOREWORD

Anchor Books is a small press, established in 1992, with the aim of promoting readable poetry to as wide an audience as possible.

We hope to establish an outlet for writers of poetry who may have struggled to see their work in print.

The poems presented here have been selected from many entries. Editing proved to be a difficult task and as the Editor, the final selection was mine.

I trust this selection will delight and please the authors and all those who enjoy reading poetry.

Kelly Oliver
Editor

CONTENTS

THAT'S LIFE

I travelled back in time today and visited the past
Things have become so very clear I know the truth at last
While growing up and in my teens I thought I knew it all
White was white and black was black I never saw the grey
It's only now as I look back I see another way.

Time and tears have taught me life cannot always be
The way that I would like it but I needed time to see
To look back and reflect on things regretting all the pain
I brought to those who loved me who no longer now remain
It's too late to say I'm sorry because they've passed away
And I must go on living at least another day.

When I awoke this morning the sun was shining through
There is still one who loves me and it's Him I'll answer to
I'll thank Him for this lovely day and live it to the full
Not going back in time again for life is beautiful.

Dawn Sansum

SEQUOIA SEMPERVIRONS
(REDWOOD TREES)

I went to see the redwood trees.
I felt humble, in their majesty,
Eagles soared over their canopies.

Millenniums have passed, as a breeze.
Those redwoods, were oblivious of me!
I went to see the redwood trees

Like magnificent giants, standing at ease,
Masters of all that they could see,
Eagles soared over their canopies.

Our lifetime would seem a moment to freeze,
Compared to a redwood's longevity!
I went to see the redwood trees.

Branches and roots, twisted to tease!
Making strange shapes, quite humorously,
Eagles soared over their canopies.

Squirrels, ran in and out of the leaves,
An enchanted forest, it seemed to be!
I went to see the redwood trees,
Eagles soared over their canopies.

E M Eagle

FIRST VILLANELLE

The lightning flashed across the sky
As my lover left to go to war
Birds to cover winging by

Would that I could also fly
Take to wings through yonder door
The lightning flashed across the sky

Heart is heavy - eyes are dry
Tears exhausted, flow no more
Birds to cover winging by

To be courageous I will try
Keep hearth and home as days of yore
The lightning flashed across the sky

The time is past for asking why
Or wonder what a war is for
Birds to cover winging by

We'll put our trust in Him on high
His care and comfort ever sure
The lightning flashed across the sky
Birds to cover winging by . . .

Joyce Alice Turner

MY HUSBAND THE WARRIOR POET

My husband is the poet without any fame
He's a disabled man, but in his heart he's free
So I thought I would tell you his name

'Eamon John Healy' is my husband in pain
Rheumatoid arthritis in his hand and knee
He is the 'warrior poet' but he has no fame

He writes poetry on things wild and tame
He also has Klinefelter's Syndrome has he
I suppose someday someone will know his name

He writes of love and hate near they came
My husband's disabled but free
But the publishers still don't know his name

'Eamon John Healy - the warrior poet' is lame
A true poet is what he wants to be
So open your eyes and remember his name

Then one day he will be remembered not as lame
As the 'warrior poet' because with this poem he helped me
'Eamon John Healy' - please remember his name
'The warrior poet' - he's wild but not tame. 2002

Joyce Healy

THE VILLANELLE

My dearest love, why did you leave?
But, life ended, for you
Now I alone, am left to grieve

As yet, I really can't believe
I don't know what to do
My dearest love, why did you leave?

I really can't conceive
How I'll live, my life through
Now I alone, am left to grieve

My faith, in all that I believe
I try hard, to cling to
My dearest love, why did you leave?

Life alone, I can't conceive
Without your love I can't pull through
Now I alone, am left to grieve

Surely God, will soon relieve
This pain I'm going through
My dearest love, why did you leave?
Now I alone, am left to grieve.

Joyce Metcalfe

DOROTHY MARY

She sat alone in a wicker chair,
My china doll, in all her array,
I washed and brushed her golden hair.

Beautifully Victorian and very fair,
Trouble was, there came the day,
Her hair fell out on that chair.

I was so sad, I do declare,
Dorothy Mary was given away,
No wig! What a fig! Sans hair!

Who will I talk to, now she's not there,
When I'm in trouble and cause an affray,
Bee-Jay listens, as he lies on his chair.

Trying hard, not creak to on the stair,
I sneak him a biscuit, hoping to allay,
After cleaning my teeth and brushing. my hair.

Truth, promise, kiss or dare,
Games my dog cannot play,
Dorothy Mary played on her chair,
Gone now forever, having lost all her hair.

Janice Mary Bodgére

BRAVE SOLDIERS

Proud and steadfast, guided by God's hand,
Through the long and weary days and each wretched night,
Brave soldiers of this land.

World War One, memorials, tributes to them stand,
Men fought with honour, hope and might,
Proud and steadfast, guided by God's hand.

Wars and conflicts, always wanton, never planned,
They fought bravely on for country, king and right,
Brave soldiers of this land.

World War Two, the foe, prompted by the devil's hand,
Our great men of war and allies, all unite,
Proud and steadfast, guided by God's hand.

So onward bold ones, as war surely will demand,
Forward now with banners bright,
Brave soldiers of this land.

Death, destruction, morose not grand,
Men with heavy hearts, for war does not delight,
Proud and steadfast, guided by God's hand,
Brave soldiers of this land.

Dorothy Chadwick

YONDER HILL

The night grows darker over yonder hill,
The sunshine waits another day,
The daylight fails; and all is still.

We saw the break of this most glorious day,
The stars now shine to cheer our way
The night grows darker over yonder hill.

We lived to do our work, our lives to fill,
We toiled all day, and on into the night.
The daylight fails and all is still.

We saw the children playing by the stream
And life should be, but yet a dream.
The night grows darker over yonder hill.

And now at last we take our rest
This night our sleep shall sure be blest
The daylight fails and all is still.

The stillness of the night is now so nigh
Sweet dreams are there to see us through
The night grows darker over yonder hill,
The daylight fails, and all is still.

Janet Cavill

ALIENS OR SLANG - WOMAN OR MAN

Writing poetry is hard for most people, but not for me
Sometimes off my tongue words just slip,
The substances of rhyming slang in me is set free;

Like apples and pears, tit willow, Rosie Lee - you know 'tea',
What's rhyming slang for spit it out - apple and pip,
I love the way the words interlock like lock and key;

Bees-keys-peas-teas or even longer chimpanzees,
Then again tip-flip-strip-pip-kip-nip and trip,
Am I talking nonsense or real live poetry?

Anyway, what is rhyming slang, but only words set free,
Dancing off your tongue like a ship on a trip,
Or the dirty old man from Dundee drinking tea;

Or the blind mice that were three,
Or my dog Basil giving you a nip,
Rhymes and songs are so like real poetry;

All the words have to be good company,
Down boy, Basil, bedtime, time for a kip,
Anyway, who wants cocoa - OK who wants Rosie Lee?

Come off it, I know I didn't say coffee,
Let's build a house of wood or brick,
Read my lips, I said tea! Tea! Tea!
I heard you the first time - hee-hee-hee.

E J Healy

THE VILLAGE DRAGON

Dragon stooping, gliding, soaring,
Over villages far below
Flames swirling, churning, burning.

Waterfalls from cliffs pouring
Down to valleys, far below
Dragon stooping, gliding, soaring.

Villagers, ever busy, bustling
Many brief lives, far below
Flames swirling, churning, burning.

Fierce marks hotly flaming
Left by the immortal for those below
Dragon stooping, gliding, soaring.

As a child, in play mice chasing
Only frolicking, this they know
Flames swirling, churning, burning.

Villagers, water over fire throwing
Turn back to the fields, their crops to sow
Dragon stooping, gliding, soaring,
Flames swirling, churning, burning.

Corinna Turner

HEAVEN'S HAVEN

I will find solace on the moor
and in the heather calmly lie
while birds are calling as they soar.

Sweet thoughts of life worth living for
imagining that I could fly
I will find solace on the moor.

Another world seems to implore
come join us drifting in the sky
while birds are calling as they soar.

Such visions I cannot ignore
with feelings too deep to deny
I will find solace on the moor.

These memories I'll keep in store
of unfurled portraits passing by
while birds are calling as they soar.

This wilderness that I explore
keeps nature's secrets locked on high,
I will find solace on the moor
while birds are calling as they soar.

Susan Greenhalgh

SPRING IN THE GARDEN

Green spears break the damp soil.
Sycamore seeds uncoil
And pale sun invites toil.

Early morning birdsong
Pushes night's sleep along
In response to nature's gong.

Hidden corners reveal
Petals like orange peel
And worms for blackbird's meal.

Floppy poppy plants grow
From last year's seeds windblown
To echo wild meadow.

Clematis clings to wall
Where soon a purple shawl
Will become a waterfall.

Once more the Earth has turned
And again we have learned
How gently we are governed.

Jeanne Jinks

THE FLIGHT

On holiday in Cornwall, on my own,
I went for a country walk alone,
At twenty-two, self-confidence is full-blown!

I passed a field of cows, all chewing the cud,
Was there a bull? My heart gave a thud;
I crept by as quietly as I could.

Glancing back up the road, I saw a brown shape,
'A bull!' I gasped, 'that has made its escape!'
I fled for my life, my mouth agape.

As I ran, I looked up, and called out aloud,
'God! God!' as if I expected His hand, from a cloud,
To snatch me to safety! Then, sweaty-browed,

I looked back again. No bull! I sank,
Relieved and breathless, on a grassy bank,
I'd had my imagination to thank!

A lesson I learned from this fi-as-co,
That God is with me, wherever I go,
And He's *real* to me - that is good to know.

Muriel Willa

SWALLOWS

We have swallows that come every year
From climes that are warmer than here,
And it's true they bring lots of spring cheer.

The reason I mention this bird
May sound to you quite absurd,
But they leave such a mess, oh my word.

We vow that each year they can't stay
In our barn where the creatures say neigh,
But they don't seem to hear or obey.

So we watch as they gather up mud
And know if we could, how we would
Let them know just where we all stood.

Our eyes on the weather vane
For late summer and the end of their reign,
Then we're left with the clean up again.

But no matter what mess the birds make
We miss them and all our hearts ache,
Till they're back from their winter break.

Patricia M Evans

Don't You Just Hate:

dripping taps
crumpled maps
toothless gaps
bad news
old shoes
long queues
smelly socks
rusty locks
hard knocks
vicious dogs
thick fogs
strenuous jogs
buzzing flies
blatant lies
shrill cries
fizzy drinks
draughty chinks
blocked sinks!

Marjorie Wieland

ENJOY THE SPRING AS IT SPRINGS

There are signs that spring is springing
The birds are cheerfully singing
This season brings a new beginning

The daffodils now in bloom
The lawns need cutting soon
Out comes the garden broom

The sun's peeping through quite bright
It adds to our delight
The garden will soon be a colourful sight

With spring just around the corner, there is no stopping
The bunny rabbits are hopping
The new shoots and buds are popping

The birds are busy in their nests
The bedding plants will soon be at their best
Now I'll mow the lawn then have a rest

Spring has sprung and the evenings are longer
With a new zest for life, we all feel stronger
Enjoy God's creation as we walk, roam or wander . . .

John Babey

OLD RED-EYE

Deep in the forest where the trees grow tall
lies the deep dark secret of a bird so small
it could lose itself in a ping-pong ball.

A long time ago when the air was clean
lived a red-eyed parrot with a stare so keen
it could stun its lunch like a meal-machine.

With a drop-dead look no prey stood a chance
when the red-eyed parrot passed a sideways glance
and put its dinner in a cosmic trance.

So just like members of a highland clan
the flock of parrots devised a cunning plan
to make old red-eye harmless as a lamb.

Soaked in a potion made of herbs so sweet
they tempted the parrot with a piece of meat
till it snored like a baby sound asleep.

Then the head-shrinker came and cast a spell
and old red-eye shrunk to the size of a snail
so that, my friends, is the end of this tale.

Susan Seward

HEAR ME

Will you be near me
I ask this with love
To pause and to hear me

In the shade of a tree
Hear the coo of a dove
Will you be near me

Please heed my sincerity
Come down from above
To pause and to hear me

To stay and yet be free
Whilst I tell of my love
Will you be near me

Now wide-eyed I see
You came from above
To pause and to hear me

To reject and to free me
I cry for my love
Will you be near me
To pause and to hear me

Pamela Bryan

LOYALTY

How does one measure loyalty?
When thoughts are never on show.
I only know you're true to me!

One has to know that they are free
And if they must, have leave to go.
How does one measure loyalty?

Love is given without a fee
And emotions start to grow;
I only know you're true to me!

Friendship is there for all to see
Makes one feel good, when spirit's low.
How does one measure loyalty?

Why can this life no better be
Than one that's filled with woe?
I only know you're true to me!

Now in peace and tranquility
I will learn to love life so.
How does one measure loyalty?
I only know you're true to me!

Maureen Ayling

FOREVER TRUE LOVE

Sometimes I feel O so blue,
'Joyce' my 'Oxford' girl please come,
Because my 'Joyce' O I love you;

'Joyce' my lover love me too,
Let our lives be full of fun,
Be my 'Oxford' wife anew;

'Joyce' your body - let me view,
From your head to your tum,
And my lover - please love me do;

And in love potions we will stew,
And I will gently smack your bum,
Slowly until one and one makes two;

And then on honeymoon me and you,
United together locked in fun,
We will go to Timbuktu;

Please 'Joyce' - please, please do,
Love me and have a life of fun,
Say you love me as I love you,
Make our love be forever true.

Eamon John Healy

AND BABY MAKES THREE

On a ship out of Dublin bound for Dundee,
I travelled with child - watching the sky,
We sailed the high seas, my baby and me;

I met a sailor - he was good company,
The tears in my eyes with tissues he dried,
Myself and the sailor and baby made three;

The captain, he married us on the high sea,
And where I was going, he asked as he pried,
The sailor, my baby and me;

The captain changed course upon the high sea,
The waves grew higher - higher than high,
Because of the storm - he made for Selsey;

It's near Bognor and Middleton on Sea,
The waves were high - hard as the sky,
But me and the baby wanted Dundee;

The sailor asked, 'Why? Why should we?'
My mother - my mother - I must try,
Well, in Dundee, your mother there you see;

'Don't worry', he said, 'we'll get to Dundee.'
Overland we travelled, past the side,
And there you and I and baby makes three;

We travelled by train past Newbury,
And kept on moving northward to Skye,
Northward we went, on to Dundee,
The sailor I met, the baby and me . . .

E J A Healy

CREATION

From nothing creation was created,
Man creates from discoveries made
Although his theories are periodically outdated.

His thoughts are strongly stated
But authenticity does very soon fade.
From nothing creation was created.

Archaeological finds are dated
And in museums they are displayed,
Although his theories are periodically outdated.

Man's hopes are often tainted
And ideas are not always staid:
From nothing creation was created.

His soundings when exaggerated
Because he knows he's been betrayed;
Although his theories are periodically outdated.

His belief in God is debated
Although the facts in nature portrayed:
From nothing creation was created
Although his theories are periodically outdated.

D R Thomas

OUR HOUSE, OUR LIFE

Sweet mystery and compounded to thrice:
Whilst living in a truly tiny place,
With a family encouraged by little mice!

When we may fly the coop once or twice,
To travel bound in places of race:
Sweet mystery and compounded to thrice.

To cultures we learn what's bad and nice:
What eloquence has a social grace?
With a family encouraged by little mice!

In the freedom we are rid of ugly lice,
Crushed by onion, garlic and mace:
Sweet mystery and compounded to thrice.

Enjoying the beauty of sun and ice,
Over mountain peaks as an airborn Ace:
With a family encouraged by little mice!

But home contained is a cake to slice,
For stuffing with glee our face:
Sweet mystery and compounded to thrice,
With a family encouraged by little mice!

Anthony Rosato

APOCALYPSE

My heart is filled with sorrow:
If what they say is true,
There will be no tomorrow.

A bitter pill to swallow,
The end for me, for you:
My heart is filled with sorrow.

Have we no time to borrow?
A day, an hour, or two?
There will be no tomorrow.

Too late to sit and wallow,
Estranged from friends we knew:
My heart is filled with sorrow.

Night must fall, void will follow,
No early morning dew:
There will be no tomorrow.

These final hours seem hollow,
There's nothing we can do:
My heart is filled with sorrow:
There will be no tomorrow.

Jim Storr

THIS THEFT OF RUIN

This theft of ruin doubles down God's eye
As the sun storms deep its red lunar glade:
This theft of ruin, doubled with death's sky

Christ's place upon earth, dreamless as the sly
Shape of the world, deems dark as bluest jade:
This theft of ruin doubles down God's eye

Predicated by death, with murder high
In a sea of hewn stream, by birth's red raid:
This theft of ruin, doubling with death's sky

Christ's life as love, dementing as the cry
Of God, unmarries death's parenting braid:
This theft of ruin doubles down God's eye

As death's worded writ brightens up the wry
Shortening of words, divined by death's blade:
This theft of ruin, doubling with death's sky

Shears the bibling mien of the seven states
Of man, descrying his dread and due shade:
This theft of ruin doubles down God's eye.
This theft of ruin, doubling with death's sky.

Jim Bellamy

THE STORY OF SEDNA

Across the frozen whiteness flew the raven with feathers of midnight
blue,
Strong wings tracing soft, silent circles in the sky,
Arcs of light, arcs of life.
Then through the hole in the mountains came, into the world,
into the Arctic
The Inuit people, who live on ice which lies
Where the air bites and crystallises your songs
And the winds lick ice on your tongue.

Some time ago, the earth still new, the tribes of the Arctic were
only few,
The Inuit building their icy igloos round,
Like the world, like the moon.
Here Sedna lived, dressed in skins and fur, a headstrong maid,
an Inuit girl,
Stroking her black hair braided and bound
She saw only shades of whitened ice, one season,
Her coal eyes witnessing blind vision.

Rejecting fine suitors Inuit bred, Sedna chose to marry a sled dog
instead,
She gave birth to puppies with kohl-marked eyes
Like warriors, like in Egyptian times.
Her horrified father in his kayak took her and threw her into the ocean,
Ignoring her shivering and shrieking cries.
In the chill, petrol water, her skin like an ice cube,
Her body hung heavy as a lead tomb.

Filled with fierce fear and anguished alarm, Sedna thrust out her
ever stiffening arms,
She tried to climb into the boat, her fingers hurting
Like rope burns, like needles.

Her frantic father cruelly chopped off her fingers, with his force,
                                                    with his knife.
Falling, falling under the inky waves and sinking
She heard muffling, a murmuring monotone,
As she struggled, sliding to the depths unknown.

Sedna was cradled by the rocks of the seabed, she became a sea spirit
                                                    or so it is said.
She loved all the colours of the fish and plants
Kaleidoscopic, mosaic.
Her severed fingers became the first seal pups, shimmying away,
                                                    sashaying away.

She is Keeper of all the sea beasts and plants,
Oh Sedna, let us catch your fish alive
But for you the Inuit do not survive.

And sometimes vengeful, capricious or angry, she leaves the Arctic
                                                    people hungry.
She locks the sealife away, leaving the Deep
Like a vacuum, like space.
Then a shaman must visit her, past Chukchi tents, past Anas
                                                    shore spirits.
Down, down, through water like dream sleep.
A comb he takes to her matted braids and cares
For without fingers she cannot look after her hair.

Into the ocean all the sins of mankind, fall and collect in her hair
                                                    as grease and grime.
He cleans and dresses it in glossy, jet plaits
Like squid ink, like porpoise.
So the grateful goddess, now graceful and grand, frees the fish,
                                                    releases the beasts,
Allowing the Inuit to eat and grow fat.
Sedna is happy let us sing in one voice
The sea is plentiful once more rejoice.

Lorraine Bare

SCENARIO

The stage is set. Drama now unfolds.
Joy, grief, hope and love are there.
Ongoing life, comes an end to love.
Curtain falls. Play is done. Darkness comes.
To death's waiting arms, I go.

Pettr Manson-Herrod

WHO?

I saw a summer sunset,
Beneath a summer sky.
I stood beside the seashore,
I gave a great big sigh!

I looked up to the heavens,
One question did I cry.
'Dear Lord
are you listening?'

'Who the hell am I?'

Tina Hoggard

JARIUS' DAUGHTER

Here in this quiet room
From the weeping world apart
Sleep just a little longer
Child of my heart.

The bloom of youth is on thy cheek
And dew upon thy brow
Oh, little maid so fast asleep
What are you seeing now?

Dost see the splendour that I knew
Ere to this world I came
And hear the holy angels singing
'Glory' to my Father's name?

Forgive oh little one that I
To a higher will must bow
And thence for my Father's glory
I must recall thee now.

These little hands in mine I take
The kiss of life I give
Open thine eyes, awake awake
I will thee vow to live

Margaret J Clark

POOR ME

I am not posh
I have no dosh
No new clothes
Shoes showing toes
Legs are bare
Tatty underwear
Scruffy hair
People stare
Going beserk
Must find work
To earn some dosh
Cos I'm not posh

Doreen Kowalska

THE FAIR

The marketplace is full,
    Not a space to spare,
Roundabouts, stalls and swings
    Are standing there.

Horns are blowing, bells are ringing,
    Music playing, voices singing,
Coloured lights are flashing,
    People rushing and dashing.

Soaring high above the crowds,
    The big wheel is turning,
Full of lively teenagers,
    Listen to them screaming.

A lovely smell is in the air,
    Coming from a hot dog stall over there,
Some children laughing, others crying,
    Ice cream and candyfloss many are buying.

Now the fair is over,
    The marketplace is bare,
Things are normal in the town,
    It will return again next year.

F Burton

THE TERMINATION

The land is blighted,
No trees, grass or flowers
Can be sighted,
The earth is dead.

Not a sound to be heard,
Not a living thing to see,
Seems that it never occurred
That such devastation could be.

Was it the carelessness of humans,
Or is it that the world became too old and passed away?
There is no turning back this time,
We and everything else has had its day.

D Field

I HAVE BEEN HEALED
(This was my own experience)

Now, being alone, I did despair,
My world had fallen at my feet,
I told myself don't cry, don't give in,
Be brave, be bold, a new life may begin.
I laid awake and looked at the moon,
My heart felt full of gloom;
The tears I had kept from falling,
Were now rapidly there without warning.
I told myself, I'm sure someone will be there
With faith and hope! I will not despair.
I turned over on my side,
My face I tried to hide,
When suddenly a voice I heard,
I raised my head to hear,
This soft voice said, 'I love you!' firm and clear.
I sat up and thought, who is there?
I'd said my prayers as I usually did.
I asked the Lord if he had come?
But realised it could have been anyone!
With this new experience I felt 'serene',
And wondered where my thoughts had been,
I do believe in God! So thought me, he had freed!
I told myself, you must have 'faith'
And God will lead me by my hand.
So, to our local church I went,
To thank God for the strength I'd gained.
I was met with greetings and smiles,
My heart was beginning to feel a little healed,
I called out, 'Oh Lord! I know your love,
Your faith and hope. I have won! Thank you.'

Patricia Hunt

TOFFEES

'I'll give thee wun . . . dun't ask agin . . .
      Ah canna think wot am doin . . .
Must tha keep movin tha jaws . . . in tempo wi me chewin'?
Nah look ere lad . . . I've arf a bag. There's plenty to go round,
It's just that these are all little uns . . . a big un fer you I ain't found!
I'll keep lookin fer wun . . . dunna fret . . . but like ah sed . . .
          I ain't found wun yet!
Thee be patient . . . I'll try another . . . cum nah lad . . . must thee
          cry for tha muther?
I'll give thee wun . . . ah told thee afore . . . so pick tha chin up
           off tha floor,
Art sure that these art the wuns yer fonder? Not the same as last lot
          makes me wunder!
That's it lad, blow tha nose . . . ah knew tha wun't like any o' those . . .
Ah cud tell by the taste . . . all lemony like . . . they'd upset tha belly
          an make thee 'skrike'!
I'll give thee wun . . . this might do . . . but to be ont safe side . . .
          I'll give it a chew!
Yer doin it agin . . . yer startin to holler . . . nah look you've done,
          you've made me swoller!
It's tha own fault . . . there ain't none left . . . I wuz thinkin of you . . .
Ah did me best . . . I'll tell thee wot . . . thee hold the bag . . .
          ah think it's only fair,
An wen yer mam buys you sum more . . . like a pal . . .
          I'll let thee share!

Laurence Eardley

REFLECTIONS

Looking in the mirror what do I see?
An image of someone I believe to be me.
Gone are the bright eyes that used to shine,
No more the smiles that once were mine.
Dark curly hair now tinted with grey,
Lines of age appeared are here to stay.
So many years have passed without a trace,
Sorrow and heartache appear in my face.
How quick the time passes, it's hard to recall
Happiness and trouble I've experienced them all.
Looking back on time, are there things I would change,
If I were given the chance to rearrange?
There were times in my life that brought me sorrow,
We can't live in the past, but look forward to tomorrow.

D Lee

OUR BITTERSWEET WORLD

In the shadows of the copse there's a million bones,
Skeletons of former life lie, to rot amongst the cones.
Birds and rodents resting, short lives, and brown, dead leaves,
The gardener takes the leaf mould, but he leaves behind the seeds.
Recycled waste to feed the earth,
This loam from death, will give new birth.

Jean M Tonkin

FIRST LOVE

I visited the place where last we met,
My feelings ran ahead.
How would my memory recollect
The things we'd done and said?

Then we were young and filled with hope,
Our lives spread open wide.
The future seemed a wondrous road,
No doubts, no cause to hide.

Why did we part for all those years?
Why feel we had to race?
I've shed so very many tears
Since we were in this place.

Memory plays tricks and we forget
The why and when and where.
But in this place where last we met
Lies still the joy we share.

Maureen Wildash

FRIENDSHIP

In all the world from end to end
I value most a faithful friend
Whose friendly word and cheerful smile
Has aided many a weary mile
Along the path we all must tread
As through our lives our way we thread.

E V Saint

SUMMERTIME SOLILOQUY

An 'ace' is not a serve, I'd say:
the serve should put the ball in play . . .
how can opponents make reply
if every ball goes whizzing by?
Miles per hour of ace times measure
flash on screen for gloating pleasure.
Are science-toughened racquets brought,
lethal weapons on the court?
Do we wait till someone falls
before we call 'aces' 'no balls'?

Helen M Cook

HOLIDAY

Matthew is going to Sicily,
I hope that he has a good time.
He's going with Ruth not Cicily,
An old name and also a rhyme.

Sicily's next to Italy
And all the men are small.
Matt'll stand out in Sicily
Because he is quite tall.

Do they eat pasta in Sicily?
And bolognese on it as well?
Matt'll have lots and his'll be
Covered in garlic that smells.

So have a good time Matt in Sicily
And don't get too drunk on the wine.
This is the last verse for it would get much worse
Because I have run out of rhymes!

Barbara Zoppi

WEBSITES

Everyone has websites,
    They find them very cool.
But they're not the thing for me, you see,
    They're just not my kind of tool.

My parents said avoid them,
    For fear of sudden death.
So I'm always very vigilant,
    And often hold my breath.

It must have been last Thursday,
    I went to see my friend.
I couldn't find the lad at home,
    He'd met a sticky end.

He'd headed off to look for food,
    Not expecting then to die.
It's a job to see those websites,
    When you're just a little fly.

Cliff De Meza

COLOURS HIGH

Bleeding colours Jacob's coat
Round and round and round they float
Saffron yellow crimson and red
Twisting spinning in my head

Pearly pulsing purple dream
Soothing moving emerald green
Carmine tears from weeping blues
Swimming mixing multi hues
Twirling slow my prism stone
Popping pills my mind has blown

Gordon McDonald

THE BED

I had a bed designed for me
It's made from pine, a lovely tree.
It has four posts and a canopy
I feel like a queen when I drink my tea.
Two mattresses it has in place
So the telly is seen with wondrous grace.
But it's getting down which brings a frown
As it's so high my feet don't touch the ground.
I slide down the side and land with a thud
Not much like a queen, more like a spud.

R P Whatling

HERE'S TO THE LADIES

What is it like to be a woman?
To have breasts that men all want to touch
What is it like to be a woman?
Men have so little - you have so much.

You can wear such lovely things
Underwear, frocks and all things posh
We can hardly get away with rings
'Y-fronts' yes - one on, two spare - one in the wash!

Stockings - that's another ploy,
With seams or patterns, perhaps suspenders
Oh goodness! Who would be a boy!
I know you win out of the genders.

If only we could understand your heads
And know what's on your mind.
But all men think about is beds
(Don't want to sound unkind!)

Enigma variations - not two of you the same
There's blonde and brown and auburn too
It's such a crying shame
But come what may (what e'er you say) we all love you.

You come in several sizes, some large as life itself
Heavy land horses, a racehorse or two . . .
You mostly want to marry - but some sit on the shelf
But size or colour, whatever, you know we all love you!

Dave Mead

BABY

Take a piece of magic dust
And a little piece of cloud,
Put it all together
And mix it all around.
Take a little miracle
Take a little love,
Add it all together
This is a gift from above.
They're given to us on loan you know
To nurture and protect,
The fact that they're not really ours
We never should forget.
As long as God has blessed us
With his angel from above,
We should cherish every single day
And smother him with love.
We should cherish every tiny smile,
Put to memory every dimple,
For the best things that life may offer,
Usually are most simple.
But most of all we must accept
This precious gift that's given
Has to be above all else
A little piece of heaven.

Deborah Jane Mailer

ECHOES

My mother says 'Stop doing that'
She's always full of moans
It's 'Don't do this' and 'Come right now'
And 'Wait till we get home.'

And on she goes just talk, talk, talk
That's all she ever does
Just what age will I need to be
Before she will shut up?

Those were thoughts I had a lot
When I was growing up
I never really understood
What made my mother tick.

Then yesterday I had a shock
I heard those words again
The 'Don't do that' and 'Come right now'
And 'Wait till we get home.'

All of these familiar words
And in a voice I knew
The world has turned full circle Mum
And I've turned into you!

Elizabeth R Davidson

TRUSTING TO TRUST

The world has changed so much today, we all have too much fear,
to stop, and chat, and socialise, to let someone get near.
We tend to keep our distance, as we seem to think we must
keep everyone at arm's length, and this shows a lack of trust.
Now why is this? I asked myself. Is this a fault of mine?
The next time that I meet someone, then I will take the time
To stop and speak, be friendly, not pass on the other side.
To show a fellow human that all trust has not yet died.
And so, when I was walking out, on just the other day,
I saw a man and spoke to him, as he was going my way.
He smiled at me and took my arm, we walked along together,
I've made his day and mine, I thought, I really am so clever!
We parted at the corner and I walked to my front door,
I went to look what time it was, my watch was there no more.
Oh no! He's robbed me, was the thought that leaped into my head,
But when I got inside my door, the watch lay on my bed.
I felt so very guilty at those thoughts I'd had inside
And after I'd been trying to show, all trust could not have died.
I'd thought I'd been so clever, been as trusting as I can,
Now I can't even trust myself, to trust my fellow man.

J Jones

TELEVISION

This is a strange box that sits in your room,
There is a constant sound made, boom, boom, boom.
Pictures appear like magic, faces on the screen,
With the brightest colours from red to green.
Quiz shows, soap operas, films you can choose,
And when you get bored, you can hit the button for a snooze.
From channel to channel, repeats of violence, shouting and shows,
It seems that the television producers think that anything goes.
Something to attract everyone from young to old,
But the producers do not care, once the licence is sold.
So in order to bring back decent television we need to make a stand,
And put our points across, let the viewers take command.

Suzanne L Shepherd

WORSHIP

To have a slice of dreams,
No matter what it takes,
To get a piece of you,
That will cure all my heart aches.

I know you're not giving it,
Not putting it up for sale,
But, to get a piece of you,
Through the snow, wind and hail,

Like no other I'd be trying,
To the bottom of the ocean I'd dive,
All to get a piece of you,
To truly know I'm alive.

I would climb the highest,
No time would I waste,
Just to get a piece of you,
I'm longing for your taste.

You keep me at bay,
No matter how much I try.
To get a piece of you,
Why, please tell me why?

I try to go without,
But you give me such a craving,
All to get a piece of you,
Otherwise I'll go stark raving.

I'd stop the mountain from falling,
I'd work the hardest labour,
Just to get a piece of you,
Your sweetest touch and flavour.

I am officially a loon,
I need you, please tell me how.
This is my ode to chocolate,
So give me a piece now!

Jamie Barnes

RETIREMENT

Exempt from military service with the forces of the Crown,
   You came to general practice in a pleasant market town.
Qualified to practise, after six long years of work,
   Followed by nights of study, you were never known to shirk.
Fate stepped in and soon the word was spread, that you were
                        dedicated to the patients in your care
   So came the offer of a partnership, if you could buy your share.

Thus you came to a large, and rambling house,
   With its scruffy peeling walls, cold stone floors and
                        all too frequent mouse.
The rooms were cold and draughty, the chairs were old and worn,
   Given by those who wished you well as you came to greet the dawn
   Of a life of service, to your fellow beings, to treat their aches
                                    and pains,
   Their ageing gaffers, and their newborn bairns.

Soon came the constant call of ringing bells, of differing tone,
   And the never silent - all persistent telephone.
Gradually accepted and welcomed to their homes
   You gained their trust and friendship, as you listened to their moans
Prescribing for their symptoms, you gave healing for their ills,
   And hated sending out their almost negligible bills.

The hospitals were voluntary, they understood the needs
   Of patients in the country, without motor cars or steeds;
It was easy for consultants to visit in the home
   And carefully identify each troublesome syndrome.
Those in your care showed their appreciation
   And never knew, or needed to resort to litigation.

Then, finding that your patients needed homes, as well as health,
  It was obvious that a voice must speak for those who had no wealth.
A tricky seat upon the council of the town,
  And a constant fight on their behalf caused many a scowl,
                                        and frown.
The days were long, and nights were frequently disturbed,
  But any feelings of frustration had to be severely curbed.

There was studying to do, and reading, to keep right up to date
  With all the changes in treatment, and drugs to estimate.
The years rolled on, the family chose to follow in your steps,
  Entering your profession, though with one or two side steps,
Each chose to serve in the community
  And giving of their best, at every opportunity.

Changes came, in every way, with computers on the scene:
  Your patients' notes thrown up, upon the screen.
This could only add to the strain of over forty years,
  Publicising as it did, all their hopes and fears.
So the time had come to hand over your authority,
  As your own health became a stark priority.

With many a sad feeling, the years of faithful service closed,
  And the reins of duty, and all the problems posed
Were handed to practitioners, young, keen and dedicated
  To follow in the footsteps, that you had once created,
Knowing that they'd bear in mind the lead that you had given,
  Taking on their duties, as you had always striven
To give the very best, and shunning any form of sloth
Always adhering to the precepts of the Hippocratic oath.

M Keeling-Roberts

DID NOT KNOW

Did not know when I was young
Life was just a song unsung
No music was composed for me
Or written words that I could see
My manuscript an empty page
'Twould be written as I age
Would the song be happy and fun
Or would it sing of things undone
Before me now so much is clear
And of my life I have no fear
For in the end 'tis down to me
To make occur whate'er will be

Hazel Mills

THE SUN IN FLIGHT

Hollying with my buddies
Rocking fumes of careless hops
Tremble kneed first Judies
Doorways private and bus stops

Smoking Merlin's moonbeams
At Lennon's magic fire
Back laid cloud floated snow dreams
Silk kited thoughts for hire

Opening buds of comprehension
Crystal dropped - one hundred proof
Two thousand years of tension
Ghost fleeted calm of truth

Jeans faded to past yearning
The speed of running sand
But the globe for once stopped turning
And listened to the band

Mind windblown like the flower
Wrung hung pegged out to dry
Beam me up Scotty - the world's gone sour
Whilst I have tasted sky

Hugh Rose

THE FUTURE

The future's getting closer, no longer just a mist.
Definitions, clear, precise,
Then becomes clear blue skies.
Past and present, no longer one, but two, separate, apart.
You're in my past, I won't look back,
Only forwards, that's where I'll be.
In the future, looking forward, that's me.

L Gill

ROUND AND ROUND

Comprehension abound
Why so many circles found
Roadways to achieve
The junction then believe
Council had an idea
It will be fine, no fear
Priority from the right
Many have a fight
Odd gesture or remark
No fun driving when it's dark
All sit round a circle contemplating
While others are anticipating
To be very blunt
There may be the odd shunt
Some bright spark will dart
When all begins to start
Some will fiddle
Others stuck in the middle
Little circle in the road
To relieve the heavy load
Not to believe one jot
It's all gone to pot
As humps positioned in street
Or sleeping policemen to be neat
Impact too hard no mean feat
Passengers at rear leave their seat
Just a thought for goodness sake
Some at the rear have a headache
Passing through leafy lanes, abound
Just going, round and round

Anthony Higgins

DO WE CARE?

Do we care if our lovely world
Is ruined by pollution?
If we do, it's time that
We found the right solution.
Riverbanks where otters play
Unsafe, unclean, unkept.
Tiny creatures dying there
In our environment.

Do we care that children starve
In countries far away?
Little bodies frail and thin,
Are left there to decay.
No food or medication
To ease their pangs and pain.
Flies in eyes, too weak to cry,
No crops grow - there is no rain.

Do we care if toxic waste
Is dumped where people live?
Canisters of deadly type
Make dangers positive.
Children play - unaware
Of perils lurking there.
People say - 'Just let it be'
And governments don't care.

If we care, about these things
Then let your voice be heard.
Protect the world of lovely things -
The butterflies and birds;
The elephant, and the tiger;
And kids who cry in vain.
Take care of all the things you love
You won't get the chance again.

Mary P Linney

It's All Gone Wrong

I am feeling very nervous, now that the time is near,
Oh help, he has just turned up, yes my new driving instructor is here,
He seems a very nice young man, courteous and polite,
He doesn't know that deep inside I am all knotted up with fright.
Mirror, signal, manoeuvre, I can't take all this in at once,
I know that I am doing it all wrong, I feel like a proper dunce.

I hope that none of my neighbours see me, kangaroo hopping
                                                    down the street,
Or that will be the topic of conversation, every time we meet.
Anyway I seem to be doing all right, I only hope that it will last.
I must remember what I am doing, as I always seem to go too fast.

Oh no, traffic lights are ahead
And I can't remember what he said.
Perhaps the lights will stay green,
No, they changed to red, and I still carried on, perhaps he hasn't seen.

No my instructor looks a nervous wreck,
And I am thinking what the heck.
Maybe I will try again next year,
As it happens I think his driving school was pretty dear.
And anyway it's not such a pest,
As I won't have to suffer the trauma, of a driving test.

Maureen Arnold

To Mum

Did what you asked of me, Mum, didn't drink.
Enjoyed my evening, we talked and laughed, didn't drink Mum.
Had lemonade and orange.
Met some new friends, nice.
Had natters with the old ones.
Didn't drink Mum.
Now I'm lying there on the floor.
Car hit me full on.
Didn't stand a chance.
Didn't drink Mum.
He did.
Now he's hurt me.
I'm beginning to pass out,
keep asking for 'Mum'.
Pains searing through my body.
Didn't drink Mum.
He keeps staring at me
saying he's sorry!
Too late now, I am dying Mum.
Wish I could put the clock back.
I'm lying here in a pool of blood.
It's getting bigger.
I'm getting frightened.
Not much life left in me now.
Feel the end is in sight.
Did what you said Mum.
Didn't drink Mum.
So unfair I'm the innocent party,
but I'm being brave to the very end.
Hands trying to help me,
but it's too late now.
Going, going, gone.
Didn't drink Mum.

Joy Bartelt

My Friends

I'm woken up early
in the morning,
by my little friends,
outside my window
singing and calling.

They sing their little songs,
even if the sun don't shine,
they'll still be there,
never late, always on time.

I always put titbits
out on the roof below,
so they always give a song
just   before they go.

Pat Block

FOR CHARLOTTE

You'll have Pepsi-Max to drink,
And throw that weak tea down the sink.
You won't wobble when you run
Aerobics will give you a tight little bum.

A Ford Fiesta's got no speed
A Harley Davidson's what you'll need.
Grey-haired grandads you will ban
And go around with a much younger man.

You won't have tight curled, blue rinsed hair,
It'll be bright emerald green to give it flair.
You won't have teeth that come out at night,
You'll keep your own both clean and bright.

We'll not see you in polyester frocks,
You'll wear Lurex tights and silver Docs.
You'll not want music without a soul,
You'll not be too old to rock 'n' roll.

You'll visit the pubs and drink red wine,
You'll bungee jump on an elastic line.
You'll dive beneath the Barrier Reef
With a snorkel 'thingy' in your teeth.

You'll not have a lap dog without any brain
You'll parade around with a huge Great Dane.
The tartan trolley will stay in the cupboard,
You'll be more like Madonna than Old Mother Hubbard.

Audrey Chester

AH VANITY!

We like your style,
Or so they say,
You should go on a mile
If only you pay,
A little to us
Before we bring out a book,
So all the fine people
Can come have a look.

And you thought it was free,
With a big fat fee,
What riddlemaree.
And who will then buy
This pie-in-the-sky?
But don't give up hope,
Though it's game,
Rope-a-dope.

Alistair McLean

DISSEMINATION OF KNOWLEDGE

In ancient times ideas spread by language communication.
Early cave drawings (14,000 BC) depicting animals confound.
Champolian broke hieroglyphic code deciphering Rosetta Stone.
Revealing tales of dynasties, beliefs, burial rites and pyramids mighty.
Deciphering clay tablets, cuneiform writing of Babylonian civilisations.
Epic of Gilamesh - stories of kings, heroes, eternal myths.

During Renaissance - knowledge spread rapidly, by printing press.
Dutch artists using camera oscura created more natural drawings
of reality.
 Far surpassing artists' creativity, capturing light and dark images
using artificial eye.
Modern photography shows more realistic views of man, his
world and outer space.
So knowledge spread by communication, writing and drawing
in the past
Internet communication uses photography, printing and sound in the
modern world.

Moving pictures - photography, adding sound, movement and light
entertain us still.
Today computer uses printer, photographs, and sounds on information
super highway -
With speed far exceeding knowledge spread by other means of
communication.

Computer invention aided by creations from artists, writers
and inventors,
Computers may generate a new art form by information super
 highway today.
For all knowledge, advances and spreads by human contact
today as yesterday.

Patricia Rosset

CEPHALONIA'S GOLDEN SUN

To Argostoli on the bus,
We travelled with so little fuss,
The sun shone brightly all the way,
And we enjoyed the views that day.

We walked along the promenade,
Where fruit was sold some good some bad,
We said hello in Greek and then,
Proceeded on our way again.

Got on the ferry, crossed the bay,
To Lixouri where the music plays.
The bands march up and down the square,
And people sit to drink the air.

Tavernas offering scrumptious fare,
A mezze plate for both to share.
A walk around the fishing boats,
And passing yachts at which to gloat.

Then all too soon return on board,
The ferry back with one accord.
To where our journey had begun,
In Cephalonia's golden sun.

John Cook

GOING ON HOLIDAY

Washing, ironing things to make
Different dresses we must take,
T-shirts, skirts and jumpers too
In case it gets cold for you.

The weather changes all the time
A mixture of clothes will be fine,
A large or small case might do
Coat, gloves and raincoat too.

The weather you cannot tell
But that is just as well,
The car is packed to the full
Just hoping it will be able to pull,
Everything is packed except the kitchen sink
We have got everything we think.

Joy Hall

HUMMING CLOUD

I look into the sky
High in the sky
And there, oh why?
Floating on high
A fluffy cream cloud
Humming aloud
To the soft country beat
So you can tap your feet
To the slow cloudy beat

Such a tiny thing
This singing thing
With its whistling hoot
It can toot along to a lovely tune
Under the moon

This fluffy ball
Is giving a puff
To a lovely lullaby

As I look up high
I wonder why? Why?
This thing as a gift
To hiss a cheerful tune
Of wonder and joy?
Oh boy!
Time for tea!
Oh lucky me!
As I went inside
I looked up high
And whistled joyfully.

Stefan Grieve (10)

POSTCARD FROM BORNEO

We're sat here in our tent
All our Borneo money spent
It will be getting dark here soon
So I've made a pretty lantern
From the torch and Arthur's hat
The creepy little bugs
Make a splendid spangled pattern
Like the spots on Mildred's cat
As they cling around the rim
My thoughts keep drifting to Hampshire
And I dream of long iced gins
The carnivorous plant life is quite attractive
And makes a glorious sight
But I feel I'm in a specimen bottle
And clammering for the light
The honeymoon is over
The bites have bruised our passion
The ants are built like soldiers
And the coffee's now on ration
Must go now dear Cecile and Jack
There's something peculiar
Moving in Arthur's shorts
And somethin' large and slimy
Sliding down my back.

Linda Doel

THE CONSTANT LIGHT

The stillness of a wet December morn
Fills me with grieving for summer days,
Winter wraps me in a dampened shroud
And sets me longing for sun-filled haze.

Bleak, deserted, puddled streets
Miss the usual patter of hurrying feet,
Instead the raindrops dance along
Making rivulets in gutters with a steady beat.

Halfway through winter's long, dark tunnel,
The pace is slow, gloomy and perverse,
The soddened earth rejects more moisture,
Floods become the winter's curse.

Yet, One there is, a birthday near,
Whose light dispels the dark of winter days,
Rain and floods will come and go,
His love is constant, here to stay!

Pat Heppel

HERE COMES THE SUN

You awake to a sunlit morning,
The first in a month or two,
It shines above the rivers and oceans,
Reflecting the shadows of the birds above.

Children running through the strands of long grass,
Over the pure green meadows,
Playing happily together from day through to night.

Lying on the sandy beach,
Sandcastles all around you,
The summer has finally come,
No one wants it to end,
And go back to the miserable cold, long days.

Jessie Coffey (13)

WATCHING SHADOWS

Watching shadows as I walk, nervously I tred,
Shadows made from moonlight play tricks inside my head.
Imagining the clouds on high, large moving shapes go by
Engulfing me in darkest shade ghostly figures clouds had made.
Under lamplight shadows small grow 10ft upon the wall
Disappearing now and then to reappear around the bend.
Unfamiliar monsters loom, I hurry through the evening gloom.
A shaft of light comes through the trees a gust of wind had blown,
The large old oak I recognised and knew that I was home.

P Evans

A Star Beyond The Zodiac

Where is the star
with encircling planet
where our like entities are,
where all thoughts we soon forget
can be found though flung
so far?

Memories deep -
so deep beyond our reach -
elsewhere, they tap in, can keep
in crater, on unknown beach . . .
wherever those beings sleep.

Do they see us
glimmer through their dreamtime . . .
curious . . . or hideous . . .
in well-sprung of sudden rhyme . . .
ever mysterious?

A long red shift
of words since time began.
We cannot traverse that rift.
Yet - for each man and woman
a planet as hidden gift.

A red shift star
with receptive planet
where our alter egos are,
holds for us all we forget
and what we secretly are . . .

C M Creedon

THE COLLECTOR

I meander on my little sorties,
seeking memorabilia from the 40s.
I wander into shops of 'junk',
seeking treasure from ships that 'sunk'.
I rummage through the 'bric-à-brac',
stuffing 'booty' in my sack.
I search market stalls and car boot,
foraging for this ancient loot.
I muse when scouring market stalls,
of antique fairs in more sumptuous halls.
Still I hope to win the lottery,
and buy some valued antique pottery.

Reg Summerfield

RETIREMENT

It's a good morning today, it's my birthday
the big '65' has come to say give up the job
and come and play.

Just to think that I can take my time
lay in bed and read all day.

What a life I am going to have
no more worrying about time.

Although this is good and I know I should be glad
I really would like to work or I might go mad.

So I will be up with the lark as per usual
and take stock of the day and do not delay
get out and about and thank the day
for I can take my time and just say this is my day.

Greta Evelyn Margolis

BELONGING TOGETHER

We were twenty when we married
And now we're seventy-six;
The years have passed like lightning
But the chemistry still clicks.
We know each other's feelings,
We hardly need to talk,
We know what are the other's thoughts
When we go for a walk.
Our children in their fifties,
A grandson thirty too
And thoughts of great-grandchildren
Soon coming into view.
We were students when we married,
Our whole careers have passed,
Already long retired and
Our work years fading fast.
We may not have too long to live -
With luck ten years or so,
But some folk reach their nineties
Before they have to go.
So let's forget our ages
And live life whilst we can,
As long as we're together
We can enjoy life's span.

D A Calow

NO FOOD FOR THOUGHT

Coming an end to this tiring day
I must take the short cut that way.
To be greeted by an aroma so light
Tickling the tastebuds so bright
For I haven't felt so hungry in a week
Just feeling the temptation so sweet.

I see the table so nicely laid,
Thanking her for an effort so paid
Hoping she's acted upon my wish
Making me my favourite dish.
I'll take her out for a treat
For she's at heart my darling heat.

Sitting by the fire so bright
Analysing today to be wrong or right,
Giving a little thought to the endless bills
My mind just hovers to the cupboard with pills
For my life is so full to the brink
I must go and take a drink.

It is true, the worst of my fears
For this has not happened in so many years.
Standing still in the hallway door
With the light so dim and poor
What came into her mind I pray
Sitting and talking the afternoon away.

Standing in her apron so blue
Giving my sore teeth a clue
Made up in so little a while
A burger in exchange for my smile,
Making me stand in my place
She sees my not so happy face.

My soul into the air springs
Showing me the goodness she brings
Taking from me my alarm
Putting me in the air so calm.
Wandering with these thoughts to bed
To lay rest my bloated head.

Samina Amjad

CHANCE

Oh the post
That comes through
The door
We are sent
Raffle tickets
By the score.

Charities, such as
Help The Aged,
Guide dogs for the
Visually impaired
But most worthy of all
For cancer care.

Our tickets never seem
To be pulled
Out of the hat
Yet someone must win
Just think about that.

Like us they
Buy tickets
And hope for a chance
To be lucky
This once.

Margaret Jenks

CATCH IT WHILE YOU CAN

Catch it while you can,
The giant billboards say;
Miss it or miss out,
The stroll along life's way.

But time - it marches on,
Determined and so quick;
One minute wrapped in blankets,
The next - old, frail and sick.

So live life to the full,
Enjoy the world around;
But a simple touch or smile,
The best you then have found.

Mark Carter

BALTIC BOUND

Some ships are tall,
Some ships are small,
And I am commander of them all.

On the wild and stormy Baltic,
I find navigation hectic -
Yet, one day, I'll brave the Arctic.

In my admiral's uniform,
Oh, what exploits I will perform!

But I am not quite old enough
To embark on a life that tough.

So I sail my paper boat fleet
On the puddles of Baltic Street.

Judith Brandon

THE FARMER

Off to bed
You sleepy heads
No reading in bed

For tomorrow is a busy day
No time for play
As you have to work all day

Fields to be ploughed
Muck to be spread
Before you sow the seeds

There's pigs to be fed
Sheep to be dipped
Before they are sheared

Then after that
Round up the herd
And start milking the cows

Have all the churns ready
So the milk can be tested
Then it can go on its way to the shops.

E Bevans

THE TRAMP

I sometimes think about a tramp
What a wonderful life he has
The open spaces are his home
So it does not matter where he roam,
The seaside front
The sandy beach
On a sunny day what a treat
Lovely parks and find a seat
Choose anyone to go to sleep
Or go and find a hidden cave
Curl up, or have a rave
No bills to pay, what a save
The sun by day is his light,
Then the stars and moon by night
People are good and kind
But he chooses this life
To be free all the time.

Doreen Day

A HAPPY BIRTHDAY TO MAURA

When Mummy was a little girl
The sky was always blue,
The fields were full of buttercups
And thick with daisies too;
And every day was sunny
And every bead a pearl,
And drops of dew were diamonds,
When Mummy was a girl.

When Mummy was a little girl
The stars were always bright,
They twinkled through the window
In the quiet of the night;
And sometimes, as she lay in bed,
The moon peeped in and smiled -
A man lived in it, people said,
When Mummy was a child.

P A Donagh

ONLY YOU KNOW

What will the future be for me?
Will I be stuck or will I be free?
Which road will I take when there's a turn to be made?
Once I've turned will I wish I'd stayed?
I'm making up my mind - no regrets.
So I'll take any road my mind sets.
I can see more clearly the path to take
But is this a dream and back to the
same old reality when I wake?
Not if you dare to start living,
you've done too much giving.
Your spirit is shining, ready to go.
When? Only you know.

Louise Hennin

SAFE AND SOUND

When I was quite a little girl,
I'd climb the stairs, and prepare for bed.
Mum would come up, and tuck me in,
And urge me to 'rest my weary head'.

Usually, I soon snuggled down,
And slipped into dreamland straight away.
But, sometimes, I couldn't fall asleep,
'Specially with doubts about next day.
So then I'd creep out from my bed,
Sit three steps down from the topmost stair.
I'd hear the 'tunk, tunk' of the grandfather clock,
Its measured rhythm easing my care.

Then, from within the sitting room,
Came the television's muffled blare.
I'd picture Mum, sewing or reading,
Or sitting, knitting, there.
Dad would be marking, or reading, or drawing,
In his big armchair.

So, having paused, and realised
That tomorrow's troubles weren't too deep,
I'd creep back to my waiting bed,
- And quickly settle down to sleep!

Robert Collins

UNTITLED

When I was just a child
I built a thousand ships
Some of paper, others bits of wood,
Some were broad and slow
Others long and narrow
These were swift as an arrow
That came from the bow.
But those of wood
Deep in the water and slow,
Soon they all sailed out of sight
Through the twisting river.
Tears stained my cheeks that night,
Father said do not grieve
Perhaps a bigger boat you'll build,
I studied, diagrams I drew
Then I built a mighty ship of iron,
When she sailed upon the river
'Great Eastern' was she named,
Isambard Brunel I was named.

A J Pullen

KIDS

Some kids do, some kids don't,
Some mums will, some mums won't,
They want to be at home,
Then they want to be alone.
They sometimes sing, they sometimes moan,
Life's never right, more often wrong,
How come life sings the same old song.

I wish they'd sing a different tune,
Do people change, only on a blue moon.
I've heard it said, mad dogs and Englishmen,
Go out in the sun at noon.

I often wonder if they stop and think,
Of what we as parents want,
Happy days, long days, a glass of wine to drink,
Relax a while, have some fun,
Think for a change of number one.

We don't have lives, just roles to play,
In this great big circle of life,
A son will always want his mum,
Until he takes a wife.
Then we are cast aside,
Without much care or thought,
We just remember lovingly,
Of all the battles fought.

Babara Johnson

LAURA'S LETTER

Your letter really touched my heart
And some what made me sad
I'm glad you had a great weekend
Your dad and I are glad

Life at times may get us down
And may not go our way
But just remember Laura
That they're not here to stay

My door is always open
On breaks to get away
Always you and Carly
Are welcome here to stay.

Ann McFetridge

LIFE

If you have a goal in life
That takes a lot of energy
That incurs a great deal of interest
And that is a challenge to you
You will always look
Forward to waking up to
See what the new day brings

If you find a person in your life
That understands you completely
That shares your ideas
And that believes in
Everything you do
You will always look forward to the night
Because you will never be lonely.

Joanne Wilcock

SEWING BOX

I have a hundred cottons
within my sewing box
but never have the right one
to darn the bloomin' socks.

I've the colours of the rainbow
and many more besides
but I can't ever find it
the right one always hides.

The spools are all unwinding
they're really in a mess
now where's the pretty pink one
to mend the baby's dress?

This button needs attaching
to the dress of red
oh bother I can't find it
I'll use the blue instead.

C Matthews

THOSE THINGS I NEVER TOLD YOU!
(To Mum and Dad)

Don't want you to ever leave me
I don't want you to ever go
Want you to live forever
Don't you leave me . . . please don't go

Never told you that I love you
Never even said I cared
Never said that I was thankful
Thought you always would be there

For all you ever did for me
For all you ever gave
Please know that I do love you
And another path I crave

Home is where the heart is
Heaven knows that much is true
I remember faded memories
And all those things I never did tell you

So before you move to pastures new
I think it's time to say
Those things I never told you
Will remain in me each day.

Lynn Thompson

A Day And A Day

I wish I could stop the sun going down on a very beautiful day.
To be able to stop the leaves of a rose from dying and fading away.
But I can keep your face and your smile in my heart
For a day and a day and a day.

The years will pass by and I must grow old
My parting I cannot delay.
But I can keep your face and your smile in my heart
For a day and a day and a day.

For you know that I do really love you
And my heart aches for I cannot stay.
But I can keep your face and your smile in my heart
For a day and a day and a day.

And when I am gone and my heart beats no more
Our love will not fade away.
For there in your face and your smile
I will stay, I will stay, I will stay.

Derek William Gresty

LIVERPOOL/LEEDS CANAL

Along the Liverpool/Leeds Canal,
The fishermen sit at the side,
Where others take a boat ride,
All enjoy their day with pride,
As they in time turn to go by.

Through the well known bridges,
Those of well known age,
As I write another poem,
On another page.

Up the canal, past Haskyne,
Part of well known Lancashire,
So much is there to admire,
Children wave their hands,
A pleasant thing to understand.

The weather truly does shine,
On this July Sunday,
 As each beat and passengers
Go merrily along their way.

Anita M Slattery

UNTITLED

Seeing your mum for the very first time
The sound that you make
When you cry your first cry.
Squeezing her finger, gripping it tight
Mum kissing you softly when you wake through the night.

Smelling your powder as she shakes it on
To the very soft skin of your tiny bum.

The warmth of her body
As she holds you tight
Mum testing your milk
To see if the temperature's right.

I am only a child but my senses are real
I can touch, I can taste, I can smell, I can feel.

Brenda Nicholson

THE BANG-BANG TREE

Have you ever seen a 'bang-bang' tree?
It's the strangest tree you ever did see,
Its branches spiral round and round,
Its roots all grow above the ground,
It bears a fruit shaped like a gun,
When the seeds are ripe it has lots of fun
Shooting them out for all to see,
That's why it's called the 'bang-bang' tree!

Kathleen Poulton

INSOMNIA

When I am tired and want to sleep
That sly old moon through the curtains peep
As if to tempt me from my bed
And seek an audience, with him instead.

All those sheep, I tried to count,
Just never seemed the right amount
To shut my mind off from the day
And forget there was no time to play.

The clock keeps ticking, the time away
While moonbeams through the curtains play
Inviting me to rise, and go by chance
To open the window, and out there glance.

On a silvery lawn, where moonbeams tall
From shadowy trees, a night owl's call
To small wildlife where on moonbeams fall
A beautiful picture, from no dreams at all.

C King

TOUCHED

Touched, touched by the news,
it was so sad you couldn't believe that it was true.
Touched, by the shockwaves it sent,
counting the cost of what we had lost,
touched and joining the growing lament.
Touched, no time for goodbyes,
so many tears and mascara streaks brought out the tissues.
She touched where no other had touched,
not afraid to tread where no one had led,
showing love, shedding light,
when she touched taboo issues.
Diana was a doer who spread, spread love around,
no matter people's colour, their age, or their creed,
she applied herself to supply their need
of help, love and understanding,
giving them hope with her comforting touch.
Touched, people said it with flowers,
notes and bouquets to express loss and praise for her life.
Touched, touched enough to ignite,
so the flame of love spread,
and the whole world was touched, touched by her love.

John Manning

NARROW ESCAPES

The little mouse quietly crossed the room
And hid himself behind a broom
He had seen the household's cat
Fast asleep on the living room mat
He didn't intend to play cat and mouse
In this or any other house
Cats can be friendly but also cruel
And this little mouse wasn't a fool
In his short life he'd had many a scrape
And each time lucky to escape
One of his brothers was killed by a dog
On that occasion he'd hid under a log
One day a cat chased his mother
He had hid in a barn with another brother
His father was caught some time ago
They'd found his body in the melting snow
His mother was left to rear them alone
Until they were ready to leave their home
All of a sudden he heard a noise
Down the stairs came the household's boys
The cat awoke and walked across the floor
And one of the boys unlocked the back door
The cat went out as was his way
So the mouse was safe, at least for that day.

Diana Daley

I WANT TO GO SHOPPING TOO

My mother's gone out shopping
But she hasn't taken me
She said I was a nuisance
And she's left me with Aunt Bea.

I've hurled my bricks
And wet my knicks
And got in such a paddy
I've shouted and spat
At their old ginger cat
And I've yelled for my mummy and daddy.

When Mummy goes out shopping next
I *know* she'll take me, for
My auntie Bea
Says she'll *never* have me
To stay at her house anymore!

E Marcia Higgins

UNTITLED

Shall I go from shop to shop
On a spending spree till I drop?
Let the train take the strain,
No, it's running late again.
There is a bus stop outside my door,
There are either none, or three or four,
By car? Scooter? Motorbike?
With walking shoes, I could hike.
Hire a boat, and set sail,
Send an order through the mail?

No need, when I can stay in bed,
And buy on the internet instead!

Stella Jones

THAT SPECIAL SMILE

I'd like to own a special shop -
People might travel miles
To peer through shining windows,
And select one of my smiles.

For piled up high, in boxes trim,
Quiet as quiet can be,
Every kind of smile would wait,
Praying, 'Oh, please choose me'.

Heavenly smiles for tiny tots,
Tender smiles for mothers,
Whiskery smiles for grandpapas,
And cheeky smiles for brothers.

Teasing smiles for teenagers,
Wistful smiles for lovers,
Grudging smiles for grumpy grans,
In jars with rainbow covers.

The price of each and every smile
Would be a frown or scowl,
Thrown into that corner - see?
Crowded cheek by jowl.

At night I'd take them to the works
Of old 'Recycling Sam' -
He'd turn them into smiles again
By mixing them with jam.

I'd never tire of sorting through
My stock of smiles for all,
But should you not be suited,
Try again when next you call.

Beryl M Smith

THE JEWELS IN HIS CROWN

He bared his all, to flash at the Queen,
But the lady was not for shocking
She'd seen all before, having borne three sons.
To unveil a statue, her reason to come
To Newcastle, a task that had to be done,
So what was the point of it all?
He ran naked alongside her limousine,
And the lady appeared amused.
The police swooped down, with a heavy arm
And soon restored an aura of calm,
The Queen moved on with regal charm
Was it worth the trouble and fuss?
It's not good manners to bare all for our Queen,
Though, the lady was seen to be looking!
His torso was slim, with a tight little bum,
To shock HM was his reason to come,
Was it worth the hassle cos all he had done
Was to show *her* his family jewels!

Pamela Carder